52 ED CHALLENGE

52 Week Guide to Evangelism and Discipleship

"It is not just an Event, but a Lifestyle"

Dr. Aaron R. Jones

52ED Challenge
52 Week Guide to Evangelism and Discipleship

Printed in
the Unites States of America

Published by Kingdom Publishing, LLC
Odenton, Maryland, USA

Copyright ©2023 by Dr. Aaron R. Jones

All rights reserved. No part of this book may be reproduced or transmitted in any form or by any means, electronic or mechanical, including photocopying, recording or by any information storage and retrieval system without written permission from the author, except for the inclusion of brief quotations in a review.

All scripture quotations are from the King James Version of the Bible. Thomas Nelson Publishers, Nashville: Thomas Nelson, Inc. 1972.

Editor: Dr. Sharon D. Jones

Dr. Aaron R. Jones

ISBN: 978-1-947741-89-8

Library of Congress Control Number: 2023921170

Table of Contents

Week 1 Challenge
Leave a tract with the next neighbor you see.

Week 2 Challenge
Leave a witnessing letter in your mailbox for your mailperson.

Week 3 Challenge
Invite a coworker to church.

Week 4 Challenge
Make a social media post inviting friends into a relationship with Jesus.

Week 5 Challenge
Call an unsaved loved one and talk about Jesus.

Week 6 Challenge
Ask the next waitress/waiter you encounter if you can pray for them.

Week 7 Challenge
Pay the bill for the car behind you and tell them God loves them.

Week 8 Challenge
While grocery shopping, spark a conversation with the stock person.

Week 9 Challenge
Buy your coworker lunch.

Week 10 Challenge
Send an email sharing the love of Jesus.

Week 11 Challenge
Offer to pray at a local homeless shelter.

Week 12 Challenge
Go tract passing with your church.

Week 13 Challenge
Start an online devotion one day a week.

Week 14 Challenge
Ask a random person if they know Jesus.

Week 15 Challenge
Offer help to an unsaved person.

Week 16 Challenge
Volunteer at a local soup kitchen and speak about Jesus.

Week 17 Challenge
Witness to the homeless.

Week 18 Challenge
Buy groceries for a family in need.

Week 19 Challenge
Wear something expressing your faith.

Week 20 Challenge
Share Jesus at your next gas station visit.

Week 21 Challenge
Give something free from your closet to an unsaved friend/coworker.

Week 22 Challenge
Spend time at lunch to pray for specific co-workers (saved and unsaved).

Week 23 Challenge
Text/email a prayer to an unbeliever and a believer.

Week 24 Challenge
Text/email a scripture to an unbeliever and a believer.

Week 25 Challenge
Write down 10 unbelievers' names and commit to praying for their salvation.

Week 26 Challenge
Pray daily that God that will burden your heart for lost souls.

Week 27 Challenge
Display scripture/inspirational words on your social media platforms.

Week 28 Challenge
Display scripture/inspirational words on your vehicle.

Week 29 Challenge
Display a scripture/inspirational sign in your yard.

Week 30 Challenge
Meditate on evangelism scriptures.

Week 31 Challenge
Be intentional by showing the Love of Jesus.

Week 32 Challenge
Donate to World Missions.

Week 33 Challenge
Donate to a local community outreach ministry.

Week 34 Challenge
Volunteer at a non-profit organization that serves the community.

Week 35 Challenge
Begin a prayer journal for missionaries around the world.

Week 36 Challenge
Pray for community initiatives that support those in need.

Week 37 Challenge
Meditate on Romans 10:9-10.

Week 38 Challenge
Be intentional about being ready to speak for Jesus (I Peter 3:15).

Week 39 Challenge
Meditate on the work of Jesus (His death, burial, and resurrection).

Week 40 Challenge
View a witnessing/discipleship video or story.

Week 41 Challenge
Connect with an evangelism/discipleship teaching/training.

Week 42 Challenge
Develop a strategy to reach someone who is an unbeliever.

Week 43 Challenge
Come in agreement with an Evangelism commitment.

Week 44 Challenge
Meditate and Praise God over your salvation story.

Week 45 Challenge
Meditate on discipleship scriptures.

Week 46 Challenge
Identify your pond (a place where God has called you to disciple/evangelize).

Week 47 Challenge
Offer to assist your neighbor in one of their home activities.

Week 48 Challenge
Leave a tract in your mailbox for your mailperson.

Week 49 Challenge
Intentionally smile at every person you see.

Week 50 Challenge
Hug, call, or text a family member you do not get along with and tell them you love them.

Week 51 Challenge
Forgive someone that has wronged you.

Week 52 Challenge
Fervently pray for your enemies and asking God to bless them.

Preface

The 52ED Challenge is a challenge and an encouragement to all believers to reach the world with the Gospel of Jesus Christ. This is a guide to lead the Church in a weekly approach toward evangelism and discipleship. In scripture, the church is commanded to reach souls for the kingdom whether saved or unsaved.

Our desire should be to reach every person, nation, *and* culture for Jesus Christ. Jesus said, *And this gospel of the kingdom shall be preached in all the world for a witness unto all nations; and then shall the end come* (Matthew 24:14).

The Church has been mandated to make and encourage disciples. Matthew 28:18-20 says, *And Jesus came and spake unto them, saying, All power is given unto me in heaven and in earth. Go ye therefore, and teach all nations, baptizing them in the name of the Father, and of the Son, and of the Holy Ghost: teaching them to observe all things whatsoever I have commanded you: and, lo, I am with you always, even unto the end of the world. Amen.* Discipleship cannot happen without Evangelism, and Evangelism is the precursor to Discipleship.

The power to reach souls has been promised by Jesus in Acts 1:8, *But ye shall receive power, after that the Holy Ghost is come upon you: and ye shall be witnesses unto me both in Jerusalem, and in all Judaea, and in Samaria, and unto the uttermost part of the earth.*

The 52ED Challenge plan is centered around the DPA Approach—Decision, Prayer, Action. DPA is an intentional approach so that evangelism and discipleship become a way of life. Each week there is a confession about the evangelism/discipleship approach; the believer prays about the confession; and finally, the believer moves into action. This is more than a plan for the believer, it should become a way of life.

WEEK 1
CHALLENGE
~~
Leave a tract with the next neighbor you see.

Decision:
I have decided to leave a tract with the next neighbor I see.

Prayer:
Dear Lord, open the heart of my neighbor, allow him/her to be receptive to the truth of Your word. In Jesus' Name, Amen.

Action:
It's your move, being led by the Holy Spirit, give the tract to the neighbor.

What is my Follow-up?

_____
_____
_____
_____

What was my Testimony?

_____
_____
_____
_____

WEEK 2
CHALLENGE
~~

Leave a witnessing letter in your mailbox for your mailperson.

Decision:
I have decided to leave a witnessing letter in my mailbox for my mailperson.

Prayer:
Dear Lord, allow my letter to my mailperson to cause him/her to think about their relationship with You. Holy Spirit, Touch their heart. In Jesus' Name, Amen.

Action:
It's your move, being led by the Holy Spirit, write the witnessing letter, and put it in your mailbox addressed to them.

What is my Follow-up?

_____
_____
_____
_____

What was my Testimony?

_____
_____
_____
_____

WEEK 3
CHALLENGE
~~
Invite a coworker to church.

Decision:
I have decided to invite one of my coworkers to church this Sunday.

Prayer:
Dear Lord, give me the words to say to my coworker to help them be curious about You, and to be interested in attending church with me. Help me to live a life that exemplifies Your Son. In Jesus' Name, Amen.

Action:
It's your move, being led by the Holy Spirit, invite your coworker to church.

What is my Follow-up?

_____
_____
_____
_____

What was my Testimony?

_____
_____
_____
_____

WEEK 4
CHALLENGE
~~

Make a social media post inviting friends into a relationship with Jesus.

Decision:
I have decided to make social media posts inviting individuals to have a relationship with Jesus.

Prayer:
Dear Lord, birth in me godly posts that will open the hearts of all my social media contacts. Holy Spirit, help me to impact them for Your Kingdom. In Jesus' Name, Amen.

Action:

It's your move, being led by the Holy Spirit, write the posts to cause your contacts to think about their relationship with Jesus.

What is my Follow-up?

_____
_____
_____
_____

What was my Testimony?

_____
_____
_____
_____

WEEK 5
CHALLENGE
~~

Call an unsaved loved one and talk about Jesus.

Decision:
I have decided that I will call one of my unsaved friends/family members and talk about Jesus Christ.

Prayer:
Dear Lord, my friend/family member needs You in their lives. I am praying for a whole-house conversion throughout the family. I pray they will surrender to Your will and way. In Jesus' Name, Amen.

Action:
It's your move, being led by the Holy Spirit, make that phone call to the unsaved friend/family member.

What is my Follow-up?

_____
_____
_____
_____

What was my Testimony?

_____
_____
_____
_____

WEEK 6
CHALLENGE
~~

Ask the next waitress/waiter you encounter if you can pray for them.

Decision:
I have decided that the next waitress/waiter that I encounter I will ask if I can pray for her/him.

Prayer:
Dear Lord, give me the boldness to speak (no matter the disposition or mannerism of the person). Let me be led by Your Holy Spirit to speak life over the waitress/waiter. In Jesus' Name, Amen.

Action:
It's your move, being led by the Holy Spirit, while at a restaurant, ask the waitress/waiter may you pray for them.

What is my Follow-up?
_____
_____
_____
_____

What was my Testimony?
_____
_____
_____
_____

WEEK 7
CHALLENGE
~~
Pay the bill for the car behind you and tell them God loves them.

Decision:
I have decided to pay the bill for the car behind me and tell them God loves them.

Prayer:
Dear Lord, give me the wisdom and guidance to choose the person whose bill You want me to pay, so that they may know You are real and want a relationship with them. In Jesus' Name, Amen.

Action:
It's your move, being led by the Holy Spirit, go to a drive thru window and bless the person in the car behind you and let them know God loves them.

What is my Follow-up?

_____
_____
_____
_____

What was my Testimony?

_____
_____
_____
_____

WEEK 8
CHALLENGE
~~

While grocery shopping, spark a conversation with the stock person.

Decision:
I have decided, while grocery shopping, I will spark a conversation with the stock person.

Prayer:
Dear Lord, direct me to the right person to start a conversation, open his/her heart to be receptive to the message You give me. In Jesus' Name, Amen.

Action:
It's your move, being led by the Holy Spirit, while at the grocery, initiate a conversation with the stock person.

What is my Follow-up?

_____
_____
_____
_____

What was my Testimony?

_____
_____
_____
_____

WEEK 9
CHALLENGE
~~
Buy your coworker lunch.

Decision:
I have decided to buy my coworker lunch and to mention Jesus.

Prayer:
Dear Lord, lead me to the right coworker. As I present this kind act to my coworker, open the door for the gospel to be shared. Let our conversation please and honor You. In Jesus' Name, Amen.

Action:
It's your move, being led by the Holy Spirit, invite a coworker to lunch and mention Jesus.

What is my Follow-up?

_____
_____
_____
_____

What was my Testimony?

_____
_____
_____
_____

WEEK 10
CHALLENGE

~~

Send an email sharing the love of Jesus.

Decision:
I have decided to send an email to a friend/family member and share the love of Jesus.

Prayer:
Dear Lord, give me the specific person whom You would like for me to send the email and share about Your love. In Jesus' Name, Amen.

Action:
It's your move, being led by the Holy Spirit, write the email to the friend/family member, share about the love of Jesus, and send it to them.

What is my Follow-up?

___

What was my Testimony?

___

WEEK 11
CHALLENGE
~~
Offer to pray at a local homeless shelter.

Decision:
I have decided to pray at a homeless shelter in my community.

Prayer:
Dear Lord, there are so many individuals living in shelters who need to hear Your voice. Open the door and grant me favor to be able to pray for them. In Jesus' Name, Amen.

Action:
It's your move, being led by the Holy Spirit, go to a local homeless shelter, and pray for the residents.

What is my Follow-up?

_____
_____
_____
_____

What was my Testimony?

_____
_____
_____
_____

WEEK 12
CHALLENGE
~~
Go tract passing with your church.

Decision:
I have decided to pass out tracts with my church.

Prayer:
Dear Lord, You know whom you want me to reach this week. As I pass out the tracts, in my community, touch the heart of those who don't know You personally. In Jesus' Name, Amen.

Action:
It's your move, being led by the Holy Spirit, go meet up with your church family and pass out tracts.

What is my Follow-up?

_____
_____
_____
_____

What was my Testimony?

_____
_____
_____
_____

WEEK 13
CHALLENGE
~~
Start an online devotion one day a week.

Decision:
I have decided to begin an online discipleship devotion.

Prayer:
Dear Lord, lead this devotion so hearts can be encouraged in their relationship with You. Let those who are called by Your name be empowered to build Your kingdom. In Jesus' Name, Amen.

Action:
It's your move, being led by the Holy Spirit, begin outlining discipleship devotions for one week.

What is my Follow-up?

_____
_____
_____
_____

What was my Testimony?

_____
_____
_____
_____

WEEK 14
CHALLENGE
~~
Ask a random person if they know Jesus.

Decision:
I have decided to randomly ask someone if they know Jesus personally.

Prayer:
Dear Lord, guide my steps and my words today to the person who needs Your peace, comfort, and encouragement.

Action:
It's your move, being led by the Holy Spirit, go out in the community, and randomly ask someone if they know Jesus personally.

What is my Follow-up?

_____
_____
_____
_____

What was my Testimony?

_____
_____
_____
_____

WEEK 15
CHALLENGE
~~

Offer help to an unsaved person.

Decision:
I have decided to assist a person who does not know Jesus as Lord and Savior.

Prayer:
Dear Lord, give me the strength and wisdom to assist this lost soul in an activity that may help them. Allow this act of kindness to transform the heart and cause them to be open to knowing more about You. In Jesus' Name, Amen.

Action:
It's your move, being led by the Holy Spirit, go to the unsaved person, and offer your assistance.

What is my Follow-up?

_____
_____
_____
_____

What was my Testimony?

_____
_____
_____
_____

WEEK 16
CHALLENGE
~~
Volunteer at a local soup kitchen and speak about Jesus.

Decision:
I have decided to volunteer to serve at a soup kitchen in my community and share the love of Jesus with those who are in need.

Prayer:
Dear Lord, guide me as I volunteer at the community soup kitchen. Grant me favor with the people that they may see my full motivation, which is to be an agent of light. In Jesus' Name, Amen.

Action:
It's your move, being led by the Holy Spirit, go to a community soup kitchen, and serve the recipients.

What is my Follow-up?

_____
_____
_____
_____

What was my Testimony?

_____
_____
_____
_____

WEEK 17
CHALLENGE
~~
Witness to so the homeless.

Decision:
I have decided to share the gospel with someone who has no place to live.

Prayer:
Dear Lord, You said the poor will always be with us, but eternal richness is available to all. Use me as a vessel to make someone prosperous in You. In Jesus' Name, Amen.

Action:
It's your move, being led by the Holy Spirit, go out in the community, and seek a homeless individual. Seek how you can be a blessing and share about the love of Christ.

What is my Follow-up?

_____
_____
_____
_____

What was my Testimony?

_____
_____
_____
_____

WEEK 18
CHALLENGE
~~
Buy groceries for a family in need.

Decision:
I have decided to buy groceries for a family in need.

Prayer:
Dear Lord, I pray for continual wisdom with my finances so that I can be a blessing to many families. As this family opens the bag, allow them to open their hearts to You. In Jesus' Name, Amen.

Action:
It's your move, being led by the Holy Spirit, go to the grocery for the family in need and leave a card with a message of God's love.

What is my Follow-up?

_____
_____
_____
_____

What was my Testimony?

_____
_____
_____
_____

WEEK 19
CHALLENGE
~~
Wear something expressing your faith.

Decision:
I have decided to wear something that expresses my faith in Jesus.

Prayer:
Dear Lord, I want to show You off to the world. Give me the right words to say when someone questions or comments about my attire. In Jesus' Name, Amen.

Action:
It's your move, being led by the Holy Spirit, find that shirt, hat, or attire to display your love for Jesus. Be ready to give a response for what is displayed.

What is my Follow-up?
_____
_____
_____
_____

What was my Testimony?
_____
_____
_____
_____

WEEK 20
CHALLENGE
~~
Share Jesus at your next gas station visit.

Decision:
I have decided to share Jesus the next time I go to the gas station.

Prayer:
Dear Lord, there are so many lives with an empty tank. They need Your Holy Spirit. I want to be used by You to fill an unbeliever's spiritual tank. In Jesus' Name, Amen.

Action:
It's your move, being led by the Holy Spirit, go to a gas station to fill your tank and fill someone's spiritual tank.

What is my Follow-up?

_____
_____
_____
_____

What was my Testimony?

_____
_____
_____
_____

WEEK 21
CHALLENGE
~~

Give something free from your closet to an unsaved friend/coworker.

Decision:
I have decided to give something free from my closet to an unsaved friend/coworker.

Prayer:
Dear Lord, You have blessed me more than I deserve, and now let me be a blessing to someone who needs to know You in a personal fashion. In Jesus' Name, Amen.

Action:
It's your move, being led by the Holy Spirit, go to your closet, and bless an unsaved friend/coworker.

What is my Follow-up?

_____
_____
_____
_____

What was my Testimony?

_____
_____
_____
_____

WEEK 22
CHALLENGE
~~

Spend time at lunch to pray for specific coworkers (saved and unsaved).

Decision:
I have decided to spend my lunch praying for my saved and unsaved coworkers.

Prayer:
Dear Lord, consecrate my lunch time with You as I intercede for my coworkers. Your Word says, the prayers of the righteous avails much. I pray for breakthrough in the lives of my coworkers. In Jesus' Name, Amen.

Action:
It's your move, being led by the Holy Spirit, during your lunch time, pray for your saved and unsaved coworkers.

What is my Follow-up?

_____
_____
_____
_____

What was my Testimony?

_____
_____
_____
_____

WEEK 23
CHALLENGE
~~

Text/email a prayer to an unbeliever and believer.

Decision:
I have decided to text/email a prayer to an unbeliever and believer.

Prayer:
Dear Lord, allow the prayer that I send today to be a source of strength to those who are in a relationship with You and a planted seed to those who need to invite You in their hearts. In Jesus' Name, Amen.

Action:
It's your move, being led by the Holy Spirit, prepare the prayer to the unbeliever and believer, and text/email this week.

What is my Follow-up?
_____
_____
_____
_____

What was my Testimony?
_____
_____
_____
_____

WEEK 24
CHALLENGE
~~

Text/email a scripture to an unbeliever and a believer.

Decision:
I have decided to text/email a scripture to a believer and unbeliever.

Prayer:
Dear Lord, allow the scripture that I send today to be a source of strength to those who have a relationship with You and a seed to those who need to invite You in their hearts. In Jesus' Name, Amen.

Action:
It's your move, being led by the Holy Spirit, send a scripture to an unbeliever and a believer.

What is my Follow-up?

_____
_____
_____
_____

What was my Testimony?

_____
_____
_____
_____

WEEK 25
CHALLENGE
~~

Write down 10 unbelievers' names and commit to praying for their salvation.

Decision:
I have decided to journal 10 unbelievers' names and commit to praying for their salvation.

Prayer:
Dear Lord, give me the names of the 10 unsaved individuals you want me to pray for. As I pray, Holy Spirit, move on their hearts. In Jesus' Name, Amen.

Action:
It's your move, being led by the Holy Spirit, start writing the names of those individuals who do not have a relationship with Jesus Christ, and begin interceding for them.

What is my Follow-up?

_____
_____
_____
_____

What was my Testimony?

_____
_____
_____
_____

WEEK 26
CHALLENGE
~~

Pray daily that God will burden your heart for lost souls.

Decision:
I have decided to ask God to give me a burdened heart for lost souls.

Prayer:
Dear Lord, Your heart is for souls. Daily, flood my heart and my mind for those who do not know You. Cause my soul not to rest until I engage a lost soul. In Jesus' Name, Amen.

Action:

It's your move, being led by the Holy Spirit, begin fervently praying for individuals who do not know Jesus.

What is my Follow-up?

_____
_____
_____
_____

What was my Testimony?

_____
_____
_____
_____

WEEK 27
CHALLENGE
~~

Display scripture/inspirational words on your social media platforms.

Decision:
I have decided to display scripture/inspirational words on my social media platforms.

Prayer:
Dear Lord, give me the right scripture and words to represent who You are and to build Your Kingdom. In Jesus' Name, Amen.

Action:
It's your move, being led by the Holy Spirit, obtain your scripture/inspirational words and post on your social media platform.

What is my Follow-up?

_____
_____
_____
_____

What was my Testimony?

_____
_____
_____
_____

WEEK 28
CHALLENGE
~~
Display scripture/inspirational words on your vehicle.

Decision:
I have decided to display scripture/inspirational words in the back window of my vehicle.

Prayer:
Dear Lord, give me the right scripture and words to represent You in my vehicle. Let me be mindful and obey the laws of the land, so my presentation will not be a hinderance. In Jesus' Name, Amen.

Action:
It's your move, being led by the Holy Spirit, obtain your scripture/inspirational words and place in the back window of your vehicle.

What is my Follow-up?
_____
_____
_____
_____

What was my Testimony?
_____
_____
_____
_____

WEEK 29
CHALLENGE
~~

Display a scripture/inspirational sign in your yard.

Decision:
I have decided to display a scripture/inspirational sign in my yard.

Prayer:
Dear Lord, give me the specific scripture or inspirational word to post in my yard. May it reach the heart of those who walk or drive by my house, make deliveries, and/or visit. In Jesus' Name, Amen.

Action:
It's your move, being led by the Holy Spirit, create the sign and post in your yard.

What is my Follow-up?

_____
_____
_____
_____

What was my Testimony?

_____
_____
_____
_____

WEEK 30
CHALLENGE
~~
Meditate on evangelism scriptures.

Decision:
I have decided to meditate on evangelism scriptures.

Prayer:
Dear Lord, as I meditate on evangelism scriptures, lead me to the ones that will cause me to reach the lost; that will enlighten, empower, and equip me to be Your vessel to those in need of salvation. In Jesus' Name, Amen.

Action:
It's your move, being led by the Holy Spirit, begin studying the heartbeat of God and meditate on soul-winning scriptures.

What is my Follow-up?

_____
_____
_____
_____

What was my Testimony?

_____
_____
_____
_____

WEEK 31
CHALLENGE
~~

Be intentional by showing the Love of Jesus.

Decision:
I have decided to show the love of Jesus with an act of kindness.

Prayer:
Dear Lord, guide my path and direct me to the person You want me to display Your love through an act of kindness. In Jesus' Name, Amen.

Action:
It's your move, being led by the Holy Spirit, display God's love through an act of kindness.

What is my Follow-up?

_____
_____
_____
_____

What was my Testimony?

_____
_____
_____
_____

WEEK 32
CHALLENGE
~~
Donate to World Missions.

Decision:
I have decided to donate to a world missions project/organization.

Prayer:
Dear Lord, as I give to support ministry around the world, I know I am fulling Your Word. Use my gift to be a witness to the uttermost part of the world. I may not be able to reach every place, but I willingly give to those who can. In Jesus' Name, Amen.

Action:
It's your move, being led by the Holy Spirit, find a worthy world mission project/organization to support with a monetary donation.

What is my Follow-up?

_____
_____
_____
_____

What was my Testimony?

_____
_____
_____
_____

WEEK 33
CHALLENGE
~~
Donate to a local community outreach ministry.

Decision:
I have decided to give to a local community outreach ministry.

Prayer:
Dear Lord, as I give to support a local community outreach ministry, I know I am fulling Your Word. Open doors of opportunities for this outreach to share the Gospel and meet needs. In Jesus' Name, Amen.

Action:
It's your move, being led by the Holy Spirit, find a worthy local community outreach ministry to support with a monetary donation.

What is my Follow-up?
_____
_____
_____
_____

What was my Testimony?
_____
_____
_____
_____

WEEK 34
CHALLENGE
~~

Volunteer at a non-profit organization that serves the community.

Decision:
I have decided to volunteer at a non-profit organization that is making an impact in the community.

Prayer:
Dear Lord, give me the strength and zeal as I go to volunteer at a nonprofit organization. May I represent You well and bring You glory. In Jesus' Name, Amen.

Action:
It's your move, being led by the Holy Spirit, find a nonprofit organization in your community, and volunteer your services.

What is my Follow-up?

_____
_____
_____
_____

What was my Testimony?

_____
_____
_____
_____

WEEK 35
CHALLENGE
~~

Begin a prayer journal for missionaries around the world.

Decision:
I have decided to begin a prayer journal for missionaries around the world.

Prayer:
Dear Lord, give me a heart to intercede for local and world missionaries. Open my eyes to be aware of the various needs of the missionary. Give me a heart of compassion to assist physically and financially. Guide my prayers to those missionaries who are feeling discourage, or lives are in danger. In Jesus' Name, Amen.

Action:
It's your move, being led by the Holy Spirit, begin a prayer journal for missionaries and start interceding. Pray without ceasing!

What is my Follow-up?

_____
_____
_____
_____

What was my Testimony?

_____
_____
_____
_____

WEEK 36
CHALLENGE
~~

Pray for community initiatives that support those in need.

Decision:
I have decided to pray for community initiatives that support those in need.

Prayer:
Dear Lord, the needs in my community are great. Send resources and support to the agencies so they can make a difference and help people to have better lives. I speak Matthew 25:35-36 into our community. In Jesus' Name, Amen.

Action:
It's your move, being led by the Holy Spirit, begin praying for your community's initiatives to support those in need.

What is my Follow-up?
_____
_____
_____
_____

What was my Testimony?
_____
_____
_____
_____

WEEK 37
CHALLENGE
~~
Meditate on Romans 10:9-10.

Decision:
I have decided to meditate on Romans 10:9-10 and keep these verses in my heart.

Prayer:
Dear Lord, allow Romans 10:9-10 to saturate my heart and life until all have encountered the Gospel of Your Son, Jesus Christ. Help me to be creative in making ways to physically see these verses and share them with others. In Jesus' Name, Amen.

Action:
It's your move, being led by the Holy Spirit, find ways to make Romans 10:9-10 known in your atmosphere. Be intentional about meditating and sharing them with others.

What is my Follow-up?
_____
_____
_____
_____

What was my Testimony?
_____
_____
_____
_____

WEEK 38
CHALLENGE
~~

Be intentional about being ready to speak for Jesus (I Peter 3:15).

Decision:
I have decided to be intentional about my readiness to speak for Jesus at any given moment.

Prayer:
Dear Lord, help me not to let a day go by that I am not mentally, physically, and spiritually ready to speak for You. Give me the wisdom needed to respond so that a change takes place in the person's life that I encounter. In Jesus' Name. Amen.

Action:
It's your move, being led by the Holy Spirit, prepare yourself to be ready to speak for Jesus.

What is my Follow-up?

_____
_____
_____
_____

What was my Testimony?

_____
_____
_____
_____

WEEK 39
CHALLENGE
~~

Meditate on the work of Jesus
(His death, burial, and resurrection).

Decision:
I have decided to meditate on the work of Jesus.

Prayer:
Dear Lord, thank You so much for deciding to die, to be buried, and to rise so that I may have eternal life. Never let the knowledge of Your work become old in my heart, mind, and soul. In Jesus' Name, Amen.

Action:
It's your move, being led by the Holy Spirit, begin intentional meditation of the work of Jesus. Daily, make time to study each work.

What is my Follow-up?

_____
_____
_____
_____

What was my Testimony?

_____
_____
_____
_____

WEEK 40
CHALLENGE
~~

View a witnessing/discipleship video or story.

Decision:
I have decided to view a video about witnessing/discipleship.

Prayer:
Dear Lord, inspire and impact my heart and mind as I view videos and stories about witnessing/discipleship. May these videos ignite fire in me to do greater works for You. In Jesus' Name, Amen.

Action:
It's your move, being led by the Holy Spirit, find videos of witnessing experiences and/or stories of those whose lives were changed by evangelism.

What is my Follow-up?

_____
_____
_____
_____

What was my Testimony?

_____
_____
_____
_____

WEEK 41
CHALLENGE

~~

Connect with an evangelism/discipleship teaching/training.

Decision:
I have decided to attend an evangelism/discipleship teaching/training.

Prayer:
Dear Lord, direct me to the teaching/training that will equip me to fulfill the Great Commission. In these last and evil days, I want to be prepared to reach lost souls. Give me the knowledge and practical application to reach the saved and unsaved. In Jesus' Name, Amen.

Action:
It's your move, being led by the Holy Spirit, connect with an evangelism/discipleship teaching/training this week.

What is my Follow-up?

_____
_____
_____
_____

What was my Testimony?

_____
_____
_____
_____

WEEK 42
CHALLENGE
~~
Develop a strategy to reach someone who is an unbeliever.

Decision:
I have decided to develop a strategy to reach someone who is an unbeliever.

Prayer:
Dear Lord, I need Your wisdom. You said, He that reaches souls is wise (Proverbs 11:30). Help me to be creative in my strategy because You created different personalities in each person. Give me Your plan for the next lost soul I encounter. In Jesus' Name, Amen.

Action:
It's your move, being led by the Holy Spirit, start developing evangelistic strategies to reach an unbeliever.

What is my Follow-up?

_____
_____
_____
_____

What was my Testimony?

_____
_____
_____
_____

WEEK 43
CHALLENGE
~~

Come in agreement with an Evangelism commitment.

Decision:
I have decided to make a commitment on the number of souls God wants me to reach this week.

Prayer:
Dear Lord, I want to reach all the people You send to me. You saved me, not just to be delivered, but also to be a vessel in reaching more people for Your Kingdom. In Jesus' Name, Amen.

Action:
It's your move, being led by the Holy Spirit, make a commitment to reach a certain number of souls each week through evangelism.

What is my Follow-up?

_____

_____

_____

_____

What was my Testimony?

_____

_____

_____

_____

WEEK 44
CHALLENGE
~~

Meditate and Praise God over your salvation story.

Decision:
I have decided to meditate and praise God over my miraculous salvation story.

Prayer:
Dear Lord, only You could look at a wretched person like me and still go to the cross. My life is and will always be found on You rescuing me out of darkness and placing me into Your marvelous light. I thank You Lord! Amen.

Action:
It's your move, being led by the Holy Spirit, start being more grateful for your salvation and recalling the story of how you came into an eternal relationship with Jesus.

What is my Follow-up?

_____
_____
_____
_____

What was my Testimony?

_____
_____
_____
_____

WEEK 45
CHALLENGE
~~
Meditate on discipleship scriptures.

Decision:
I have decided to meditate on discipleship scriptures.

Prayer:
Dear Lord, You are looking for me to be a vessel of multiplication for Your Kingdom. In Your Word, teach me how to use wisdom with others to encourage the importance of being in a relationship with You. Give me the ability to train people to live for You. In Jesus' Name, Amen.

Action:
It's your move, being led by the Holy Spirit, begin meditating on discipleship scriptures daily.

What is my Follow-up?

_____
_____
_____
_____

What was my Testimony?

_____
_____
_____
_____

WEEK 46
CHALLENGE
~~

Identify your pond (a place where God has called you to disciple/evangelize).

Decision:
I have decided to find my pond (the place where God has called me to disciple/evangelize).

Prayer:
Dear Lord, show me my pond. Take me to the place where You want me to reach lost souls and disciple those who have a relationship with you. In Jesus' Name, Amen.

Action:
It's your move, being led by the Holy Spirit, identify your pond, and begin to evangelize and disciple.

What is my Follow-up?

_____
_____
_____
_____

What was my Testimony?

_____
_____
_____
_____

WEEK 47
CHALLENGE
~~

Offer to assist your neighbor in one of their home activities.

Decision:
I have decided to assist my neighbor in one of his/her home activities.

Prayer:
Dear Lord, direct me to the neighbor whom you want me to reach. Open my neighbor's heart to be receptive to the help. Grant me an opportunity to share the gospel. In Jesus' Name, Amen.

Action:
It's your move, being led by the Holy Spirit, go to your neighbor, and offer your assistance to clean their yard, garage, or in their house.

What is my Follow-up?

_____
_____
_____
_____

What was my Testimony?

_____
_____
_____
_____

WEEK 48
CHALLENGE
~~
Leave a tract in your mailbox for your mailperson.

Decision:
I have decided to leave a tract in my mailbox for my mailperson.

Prayer:
Dear Lord, show me the exact tract that will reach the heart of my mailperson. Stir the mailperson's heart to be curious to know more about You. In Jesus' Name, Amen.

Action:
It's your move, being led by the Holy Spirit, place the tract in your mailbox and address it to him/her.

What is my Follow-up?

_____
_____
_____
_____

What was my Testimony?

_____
_____
_____
_____

WEEK 49
CHALLENGE
~~
Intentionally smile at every person you see.

Decision:
I have decided to intentionally smile at every person I see.

Prayer:
Dear Lord, You have given me so much to smile about. To have a frown seems almost sinful. Help me not to hold back my smile, so it can be contagious to this dark world. In Jesus' Name, Amen.

Action:
It's your move, being led by the Holy Spirit, intentionally start smiling at everyone you see.

What is my Follow-up?

_____
_____
_____
_____

What was my Testimony?

_____
_____
_____
_____

WEEK 50
CHALLENGE
~~
Hug, call, or text a family member you do not get along with and tell them you love them.

Decision:
I have decided to hug, call, or text a family member that I do not get along with and say, "I love you."

Prayer:
Dear Lord, restore the relationship in my family that have hindered, damaged, or separated us. Be in the midst of my communication with them. May the outcome bring You glory and honor. In Jesus' Name, Amen.

Action:
It's your move, being led by the Holy Spirit, contact that family member you do not get along with and say, "I love you."

What is my Follow-up?

_____
_____
_____
_____

What was my Testimony?

_____
_____
_____
_____

WEEK 51
CHALLENGE
~~
Forgive someone that has wronged you.

Decision:
I have decided to forgive someone that has wronged me.

Prayer:
Dear Lord, You have forgiven me on countless times in my journey. You said in your Word that we should not count the number of times someone has wronged us (Matthew 18:21-22). Help me to forgive every time and to love at all times. In Jesus' Name, Amen.

Action:
It's your move, being led by the Holy Spirit, start forgiving those who have wronged you.

What is my Follow-up?

_____
_____
_____
_____

What was my Testimony?

_____
_____
_____
_____

WEEK 52
CHALLENGE
~~

Fervently pray for your enemies and asking God to bless them.

Decision:
I have decided to fervently pray for my enemies and asking God to bless them.

Prayer:
Dear Lord, You are the ultimate example of praying for Your enemies. You have given me the mandate to pray, to bless, and to do good to them who despitefully use me (Matthew 5:44-46). Help me to be obedient to Your Word. In Jesus' Name, Amen.

Action:
It's your move, being led by the Holy Spirit, start fervently praying for your enemies and asking God to bless them.

What is my Follow-up?

_____
_____
_____
_____

What was my Testimony?

_____
_____
_____
_____

Salvation Prayer

The Sinner's Prayer is for everyone who does not know Jesus Christ as his Lord and Savior. This prayer contains all of the key elements of Romans 10:9. When the unbeliever is tired of his/her lifestyle; when it seems that there is nowhere else to go; when life's trials are overwhelming, the sinner's prayer is the cure:

Lord, I am sorry, and I repent of all my sins (known and unknown). Lord, please forgive me of all my sins and wash me whiter than snow. I confess that you are Lord and Savior. I believe in my heart that you died on the cross for my sins. I believe in my heart that you rose from the dead on the third day. I believe You are coming back for me. I thank you, Lord, for another chance.

In Jesus' Name, I pray, Amen.

Author Bio
Dr. Aaron R. Jones

Dr. Aaron R. Jones serves as Senior Pastor of New Hope Church of God of Waldorf, Inc. He oversees New Hope COG World Missions which provides mission support to Jamaica, Indonesia, Africa, Philippines, Zambia, and Europe. Dr. Jones also oversees New Hope Church COG Ghana, New Hope COG Uganda, and New Hope Naga Philippines Outreach Center.

Dr. Jones serves on the International Church of God's Ministry to the Military Board. He also serves on the DELMARVA-DC Regional Council; Coordinator for the Ministerial Internship Program; Chairman of the Ministerial Development Board; and Chairman of the Intercultural Advisory Committee.

In his local community, he is the Executive Director of New Hope Community Outreach Services, Inc, a nonprofit organization that provides human services to residents in Charles County, Maryland, and the surrounding communities. Dr. Jones serves as a Chief of Chaplains for the Charles County Sheriff Office; Board Secretary for the United Ministers Coalition of Southern Maryland, Inc.; Board Member of the VConnections in Waldorf, MD; Co-Chair of the Religious Affairs Committee of the Charles County NAACP; and Charles County Community Mediator.

Dr. Jones earned a Doctorate in Theology and Pastoral Counseling from Life Christian University and a Doctorate in Christian Counseling from American Christian College and Seminary. He is a Certified Pastoral Counselor with the International Association of Christian Counseling Professionals and a member with the International Coach Federation. He is a Certified SYMBIS Facilitator, a Certified LeaderLabs Trainer, and TTI Success Insight 12 Driving Forces and DISC Certified.

Dr. Jones is the Founder and Owner of God's Comfort Ministries (GCM) based in Waldorf, MD. GCM provides Christian literature, leadership, coaching, evangelism, discipleship, and soul care training. He has published 39 books/workbooks and has recorded two CDs.

Dr. Jones not only serves God, but he also served his country as well. He served over 20 years in the Armed Forces. He is a retired Chaplain with the Army National Guard. He participated in both Operation Noble Eagle (2003) and Operation Iraqi Freedom III (2005). With all his accomplishments, Dr. Jones is happily married to his wife, Sharon, for 26 years.